The End Of Time

By Derrick Whitsy Jr

Copyright 2017

The End Of Time

Disclaimer

Ordering Information:

Quantity sales. Special discounts are available on quantity purchases by corporations, associations, and others. For details, contact the Author at the contact info above.

Printed in the United States of America

Table Of Contents

Introduction

There are a number of very serious things on the agenda that are to to transpire for this year and these next few years to come. Therefore this book is meant to give you a foundational understanding of these things. Some of you may be well versed in the subject matter already, and others of you are not, to which, in a case like this, most people are not familiar with these sorts of topics. And the worse part of that is the fact that many of these same people do not even care to know the truth of these matters. Then you have those who are the perpetrators of these things, placing stumbling blocks before humanity, leading them astray and destroying them.

Such is the climate of the world that we live in today, yet I understand all too well Who The True Orchestrator of these events Are. It is only by the Grace of God that your eyes are opened to the material that is to be revealed in this book. God picks and chooses whom He Wills that will receive these truths, for it is the difference between eternal life and death. Although God desires all of us to be Saved He wants to know where your Heart is. Do YOU desire to be Saved? Do you know that you need Salvation? Or are you one of those that reject Him,?, Uncertain perhaps?, on the fence? You, the reader fall into one of those categories, unless of course you are already Saved.

Salvation is what it all comes down to dear friends. Do you know Yeshua as your Lord and Savior? Do you believe in your heart, and have you confessed with your mouth that Yeshua is the Son of God, and are you living according to God's Word.?. This is some very serious stuff to consider and keep at the fore front of our thoughts, seeing as how all the things to be discussed concern the very fabrics of us human's livelihood. And if you happen to be a perpetrator of any of the things mentioned in this book, I will most certainly be praying for you, as I have been. Somebody has to be the bad guy right?

But my Father is able to save to the utmost, and this is your invitation as well, into His Kingdom. I understand that the publishing of such material as this has the tendency of bringing about various "controversies" about the individual whom published the material, which is due to the fact that the perpetrators of the information are afraid of the masses "waking up" and thwarting their agenda. The other angle is from some prideful scoffish camp within the masses who would try and discredit my work. Either way, Yahweh is in control and it is He who allows or disallows anything to/from happening to anyone at any time. This is about much more than just exposing a bunch of wealthy evil people, they are but a peace in God's grand design of how the operates and how it is to come to an end.

Although they will be discussed to some degree throughout this book, do understand that my focus and purpose in life is greater than just subject matter(s) regarding these people. At this point, to even discuss these sorts of things is just casual conversation to me, therefore take no offense to my words, even if you just so happen to be one of the perpetrators reading this book. I understand and know already that no matter how much information me and other people put out concerning these things, that most people are STILL no going to get it, and that is the reality that we live in today. The elite have done an absolutely splendid job at brainwashing the masses, quite the genius work if I may add. Billions of lives hang in the balance, thus God has ordered few of us to sound the alarm and reach out to the masses with His Word/Message/Truth.

I have no personal qualms or quarrels with anyone for life is too short to hold grudges, yet I do say if anyone has a problem with me or what I've said, in any way please feel free to address me on the subject matter and let's see what form of understanding we can bring about regarding the matter. No matter what your position of power, wealth, or authority you have in this world, the contents of this book concern your life. No one is exempt from the Judgment of God, and He doesn't require that you believe in Him for you to still be Judged by Him. But there seems to be a thickening air of pride and resentment amongst the inhabitants of the world, against God, the true God, as if, there is no 'reward' for such an attitude. Although I will say, there is the mass conditioning and subtle warfare which has been perpetuated on to the people for thousands of years, which plays an enlarging role in such a costly attitude.

Blasphemous lies having been passed down through the years against God, and all things regarding His truth in the world, which has led many astray and onto the broad path of destruction. Even self-professing Christians, my fellow ("former") Brethren in Christ, whom have been washed away from the truth by the lies of this world into false doctrines. It amazes me the things which I've come across over the years, mainly on Facebook, which is one of the best places hands down to gather information on people's beliefs. And there is some straight up far out there doctrines that are not even worth entertaining most of the time.

The reason for this is that most people are in the world and without God in their lives. Subsequently they don't have His Spirit inside of them Via Yeshua, therefore are void of the freely given Eternal Truth and Life that God desires all of us to have. Billions of people will perish in the coming Tribulations that are to come upon this world and it will be a very perilous time in history for us all. One can only pray that to be shielded from these things and to have the wisdom to make the right decisions. God wants to know the truth, he wants to give us instruction but we must be tuned into Him, for He will not force Himself onto anyone.

Another thing to note, are the people who like to call all of this material being presented, "Conspiracy Theories". My heart really goes out to those people as they are in for perhaps the Rudest Awakening yet. I rarely ever even entertain such statements anymore as they are not even worth the time unless I feel God leading me to speak into their lives. Usually it is the people who are the most "educated/intelligent" who like to say such things. This is the year 2017, and there is information literally all over the place in regards to the subject matter being mentioned beyond this point.

Just about everyone has access to a supercomputer, ie, your smartphone, so there's very little excuse on why a person doesn't know about any of these things, other than having dangerously misplaced priorities. Or if you happen to have been living in some far off remote location of the world. But I also tend to forget, as I mentioned before, that it is God who picks who's eyes he wants to open up. Him opening up a person's eyes is also determined by that person's heart; do they have the heart to know the truth; do they genuinely desire to know the truth? These are very important questions to ask your self.

Cognitive Dissonance is a very real thing and most people experience that when these sorts of things are revealed to them. So if you are one of the few whom are able to receive this receive this information then you are truly blessed, for the fact of the matter, the sad truth of it all, is that most people will not get it. People perish for a lack of knowledge and this is one of those things where knowing about it makes all the difference in the world in how you live your life. It's too late to prepare for anything when the S is already hitting the fan. Please understand what I am saying to you dear people.

If you've read my book, Prophetic History Within Our English Alphabet, then you may notice the striking similarity between this book and the "End Times" section of that book; that's because this book is entirely based off of that section, as is the case with a few other books that I've written that are based off of that same book. I wanted to do this to add to my End Times Ministry product line and just because this material deserves its own book anyway. So by having it in the Prophetic History book first, it made it much easier to "make" this book. A simple copy, paste, and edit, made this book much more streamlined to complete in a decent amount of time. I also have a separate, "Surviving The End Times" survival guide that I've put together for people to have something to refer to for their knowledge of being able to prepare for the end times disasters ahead.

If you have genuinely and diligently searched for the truth concerning global affairs and world history, has really done some thorough research, even if you're NOT a believer in Jesus Christ, there's simply no way possible that we could not be on the same page when it comes to these things. Especially when we have very powerful men and women PUBLICLY confirming/ verifying the very same things that us "conspiracy theorists/kooks/insert nonsense here" have been saying for several generations. Ignorance is a choice in these days, and when we have such world shifting events transpiring right before our eyes, it becomes extremely hard to not see what is really going on. It is time to awaken from your slumber dear people! Turn the TVs OFF, the video games OFF; stop allowing yourselves to be brainwashed by the wickedly propagated BS that has plagued the people of this world for so long.

Chapter 1

Spiritual Wickedness In High Places

God the Father, Yahweh, created all things through His Son Yeshua, and it is He who is the supreme Authority or heaven, earth, and hell, and it is he who will judge the inhabitants of the world past and present on the day of Judgment. Yahweh has allowed Lucifer and the rest of the fallen angels to "rule" and war against the world since they were kicked out of Heaven. And since then, satan has continuously persecuted human kind in a multitude of ways. But, he can't do anything without God first allowing it to happen; satan must obtain permission from God before he can carry out His plan(s) on the earth. God tells us in His Word that we wrestle not against flesh and blood but against spiritual wickedness in high places, and indeed that is what it is.

As exampled all throughout the Bible and all over the world today, and throughout history in general; when a nation is disobedient to God, He hands them over to wicked leadership. Not only will God give them over to corrupt leadership, but He will also send them into captivity, war, genocide, natural disasters, etc. My Father is very creative in how He chastises people, but the odd things is, people see these things happening and have resentment towards God, as if, He's not supposed to Judge people, as if, since He's God He should "maybe instead" just snap His fingers and make everything alright instantaneously. Well, the obvious reality is that it just doesn't work like that. God has ordained His standards, His Laws and statutes in the earth

15

for us humans to abide by. But the thing about it is, God does not and will not force anything on us.

And with that being the case He gives us ample opportunity to repent and seek Him with a genuine heart. If the people don't, that then gives satan the legal authority to come in and have dominion over the people and oppress them, which has been evidenced all throughout history. Tyrannical dictators who have nothing but ill intent for the people in mind, oppressive policies and laws, etc. But even in those worse case scenarios, God yet still provides a way out for those that will seek Him in those times. As I mentioned before, He is certainly a gentleman, and we know that he has no problem sitting back and watching a nation consume itself in its own lusts.

Now, specifically, concerning the 'Spiritual' Wickedness In High Places; God has allowed the Kingdom of Darkness to have a form of 'Rulership' over the Earth, as in, through the Satanic leadership of the world, the most 'powerful and elite' leaders. Those who sit in positions of power above the various governments of the world. We know that these spiritual forces are the ones who really pull the strings on the earth and that the humans on the earth whom possess this "power" are merely pawns for these entities. Quite a fascinatingly sad story for these people, having to live under the thumb of the Satan, at his becking call all of their lives. Its important that we pray for the souls of them as well, for we know that where people like that end up, no doubt about it.

The problem with this is, they believe that they are right and we are wrong. To elaborate, their God is Lucifer, literally, the same guy that betrayed God and was kicked out of heaven alongside his followers. And now he has successfully convinced these wickedly evil individuals that God, Yahweh, is the bad guy and was wrong for what he did, and that Lucifer is right and justified in his ways. Such of these people have the plot, not 'ironically' a Biblical plot, to destroy the world and depopulate the earth, which will be discussed in greater detail later on in this book. But please do take note of the paralleling correlation between God's Word and how the wicked are doing exactly what God said would happen.

The satanic elite are only doing what they have been commanded to do by their false god Lucifer. The Kingdom of Darkness has a chain of command just like any other earthly organization does. There are rankings of demonic forces and there many more of them than there are of us. They operate in what is the 2nd Heaven, which is a vast thick dark cloud that covers the earth and is inside of the spirit realm. From this base of operations the demons are sent to various locations around the earth to carry out a multitude of evil things against us humans.

The human power structure of today is quite evident and very hard to miss. There are a number of very powerful families that have this 'dominion' over the earth through various institutions, agencies, and corporations. Their ultimate goal is to have us humans living under a Plutocratic Communistic society. A land ruled by the Elite and everyone else is a slave living in a abject poverty and any and all of our property belong to them, which, is already somewhat the case in the world today. These 'Elite' families are the most evil people in the world and are even prideful about it, as if, there will be no consequences whatsoever for their actions; as if, God isn't keeping a record of all of our works or they won't have to answer for any of their doings and will get a free pass when it's all said and done.

But I must say, these people were my greatest inspirations in life. They inspired me to be more ambitious for God, and to take my walk with Him to the next level.

Specifically, it was the Rothschilds family that inspired me; I had never found so much inspiration in my entire life until I learned about these people. This family is one of those whom the governments of the world are in debt too, the International Bankers, the owners of the Federal Reserve, etc, alongside Rockefellers, Morgans, Warburgs, Saxe Coburg Gothas, Windsors, Bushes, etc etc, and the list goes on. It is quite a feat to have the masses in a perpetual state of gullibility for so long.

And as my understanding of these events grew and matured, I learned that it couldn't be anyone BUT God who is the ultimate Author of these things. There's just no other conclusion; it would be impossible for things to happen any other way outside of a God ordering these things into existence. Now I've began more and more to see it as the perfectly flawed system that is. One can see God's Fingerprint Of Creation, but can also see mankind's erroristic dealings with it. God told us in His Word that it is He who turns the heart of the King; his heart is in God's hand, and God can do whatever He desires with it.

History has shown this all too much; as discussed earlier, in regards to the disobedience of a nation, Israel, for example, perfect example of how God deals with such acts. On several occasions, due to the Children Of Israel's disobedience, God allowed them to, lose wars, get robbed, taken into captivity, He gave them evil leadership, etc; He made no exceptions! And that clearly has not changed. The world today is more corrupt 'perhaps' than it ever has been., as God tells us in His Word, as in the days of Noah, so shall it be when the Son of man returns. In the days of Noah, it was extremely evil, and God was hurt by what humanity had become.

This was largely due to the fact that the Watcher Angels of God had mated with the women on the earth, taught them 'secrets' which they didn't need to know, and thus the spiraling downfall of humanity began, although sin had already been present. The Angelic mingling with humans simply accelerated the rate and type of evil that was committed, to which, was abomination in the sight of God. The Nephilim were born as a result of the intermingling of the species, men and women who grew into giants. Not only this, but as history tells us, these giants turned on the humans and began to war against them, causing much destruction in the land. These things heavily provoked the anger of the Lord, so He cleansed the world of this evil by flooding it.

This bloodline the Nephilim still continues to this day and can be found among the elite rulers of the world. They have taken very diligent care to preserve their bloodline, by way of incestuous relations with their own family, as a means of keeping the wealth and power inside the family. On a few occasions there has been some 'other' family relations to create/form different hybrid bloodlines between amongst them. It's quite the sickening fact of matter that we have here in the world today, very disgusting to say the least; the sheer desperation of these people to perform such

24

blasphemy is just astounding. But speaking from the spiritual perspective, I understand how and why these things have come to be.

Chapter 2

Blood Moons

Most times in history when there's ever been a Blood Moon, Something significant would happen with the nation of Israel. Yes, there is a "scientific" reason for these Blood Moons occurring, but there is first and foremost a spiritual reason behind these happenings. God tells us repeatedly in His Word that there will be signs in the Heavens to alert us to different things happening in the world. So lets' take a look at a few events what have happened to the nation of Israel in the past when a Blood Moon Occurred : Note : All of them have fallen on the first day of the Jewish Holidays Passover and Sukkoth.

1493 : Spanish Inquisition : Blood Moons:
April 2nd, and September 25th. The final
year of the Spanish Inquisition was in 1492.
This event was lead by Tomas de
Torquemada and is one of the most
catastrophic events to affect the Jewish
people.

*Several thousand Jews died during this
time period. Around 200,000 were expelled
from Spain in 1492.

**1948 : The War Of Independence For
Israel :**

Blood Moons : April 13, 1949 and October
7, 1949.The Arab – Israeli War That
happened May, 1948to March of 1949 was
a very important landmark in Israel's
History. The war lasted for 9 months with
Israel being the Victor.

1967 : The Six Day War : Blood Moons:
April 24 and October 18.

Tensions between Israeli and its neighboring countries got very bad again, which caused Israel to launch a pre-emptive strike on the Egyptians and various other surprise attacks. The war lasted 6 days until a ceasefire was signed. The opposing countries lost several thousand soldiers while Israel lost under a thousand.

2015 : Blood Moons : April 4th, and September 28th

Both of those Blood Moons fall on Jewish Holidays. Passover and Feast Of Trumpets, respectively. The Peace Treaty Between Israel and The Arab Nations will be signed soon, but when?

Notice something else that is happening alongside this. On September 22 – 27, **2015**,

Pope Francis will be In America for the first time, in Philadelphia. Right BEFORE the last Blood Moon of this year.

His purpose for being in America, is to "Unify" the Catholics and The Non Catholics.

Now if you know what the Bible says, you will know that this most definitely spells the End Of It All. For when they shall say "Peace and Safety", sudden destruction shall come upon them. This is not to say that the Pope will come here and say "Peace and safety", but it is to say that we most certainly are in for the ride of our lives from that point on.

Below are 3 scriptures in which God tells us about the sun being turned into darkness and the moon becoming as Blood before He returns to the Earth. These cosmic

29

signs are definite indicators that His return is imminent. Having said that, "many" of us are aware of the past Blood Moons which have already taken place; which may cause some to doubt even more the validity of Jesus coming back anytime "soon". The scoffers must behaving a field day with this I can imagine; "With all of these Blood Moons, why hasn't He returned yet?"

As with all things that pertain to God, Spiritual Matters such as these are understood with Spiritual Eyes via the Discernment of the Holy Spirit. And even with that, sometimes even the Brethren In Christ miss the mark in proper Discernment at times. We must be completely led by the Holy Spirit so as to minimize the human error component to understanding God's Word.

Joel 2 : 31; "The sun shall be turned into darkness, and the moon into blood, before the great and the terrible day of the Lord come."

Acts 2 : 20; "The sun shall be turned to darkness, and the moon into blood, before that great and notable day of the Lord come."

Revelations 6 : 12; "And I beheld when he had opened the sixth seal, and, lo, there was a great earthquake; and the sun became black as sackcloth of hair, and the moon became as blood;"

As you can see here, the Lord makes it clear that He will return after these notable signs in the Heavens. There were 2 in the year 2014, and in 2015, there were 2 more Blood Moons, one on April 4th and the last one on September 28th. We must also use discernment on these events as well; there isn't going to always be something to happen when this phenomena occurs, thus, as by default, we must be lead by the Spirit of God when searching for the truth concerning these things.

Chapter 3

Economic Collapse

Economic Collapse is just another form of chastisement by God to an unrepentant nation of people. Currency Crisis, Droughts, Commodities shortages, stock market crashes, are all cleverly designed and orchestrated in some way to punish some group of people somewhere. And as fate would have it, as God has designed it, these economic collapses, and other calamitous events, happen on a systematic basis. In the Book Of Leviticus, Chapter 25, verse 2, God told Moses to tell the children of Israel, "When ye come into the land which I give you, then shall the land keep a Sabbath unto the Lord.

3. Six years thou shalt sow thy field, and six years thou shalt prune thy vineyard, and gather in the fruit thereof;

4. But in the seventh year shall be a Sabbath of rest unto the land, a Sabbath for the Lord: thou shalt neither sow thy field, nor prune thy vineyard.

5. That which groweth of its own accord of thy harvest thou shalt not reap, neither gather the grapes of thy vine undressed: for it is a year of rest unto the land.

6. And the Sabbath of the land shall be meat for you; for thee, and for thy servant, and for thy maid, and for thy hired servant, and for thy stranger that sojourneth with thee.

7. And for thy cattle, and for the beast that are in thy land, shall all the increase thereof be meat.

And from that point on God goes on to explain the Jubilee years, which are 7 Sabbaths, which is 49 years. If you want more information on this particular discovery, google Johnathan Cahn.
God has really blessed him with eyes to see. So, as it turns out, these Sabbath years have a parallel impact on the Global Finance/ Geo-Political Arena. Every 7 years, some form of Economic Collapse or major significant event happens in some region of the world. The past 2 have, and a number more preceding those, have taken place in America.

2015 :::: The current American debt is over 18 Trillion Dollars. A Number of other countries are going outside of the US dollar dominated system, which has plagued the world for so long. The biggest component to this system being, the Petrodollar. Counties purchasing oil from Saudi Arabia, would have to use US Dollars, which has created an Artificial demand for US Dollars. There are a number of other Geo-Political factors at play that's not included in this book.

2008 :::: Housing/Stock Market Collapse

2001 :::: Internet Bubble/Stock Market Collapse

1994 :::: The Mexican Peso lost 50% of its purchasing power.

1987 :::: "Black Monday"/Stock Market Crash

And every 7 years before that was market collapse, or some other significant event to transpire. So here in this current year, we are right on schedule for another collapse. This has to be the final collapse before the Antichrist is revealed. It is speculated by many, including myself, that this will be more worse than the Great Depression. This is all just music to the ears of the Elite Bankers and Spiritual Powers of the world. They work behind the scenes against the interests of the people of the world, and has for centuries used money to enslave them.

The Ultimate End Goal is to Collapse the World Economy via Currency Wars and the Blatant Mishandling Of Massive Sums Of Money, And Force Every Citizen To Accept the completely electronic RFID Chip. This "Chip/New Technology", will be the Mark Of The Beast. This is stated in Revelations 13 : 16 ;

"And he causeth all, both small and great, rich and poor, free and bond, to receive a mark in their right hand, or in their foreheads:" You will not be able to operate in the world economy unless you have this Mark. This will be "promoted" as the newest most "breakthrough" form of technology up until it becomes mandatory for everyone to receive. Do not be deceived dear people.

In Order for this to happen the global economy must first be collapsed. How will this happen? America will play a major role in the global economic collapse. It's Federal Reserve system, alongside the rest of the evil central banks and their "money masters", which has caused destruction for many years around the world, will fall apart and take the rest of the world with it. A big part of this fraudulent operation is the fiat currency system which has been in place for a very long time now. There are other factors and Geo-Political circumstances

besides this that will play a part in this.
Research people and no longer live in
the dark as to what is happening around you.
These topics being mentioned require your
immediate attention.

If you look at what is happening in
the financial markets around the world right
now, and you know how to connect the dots,
you will see that we are in fact facing an
inevitable global economic meltdown. This
will begin in America this year. America
utilizes a fraudulent fiat currency monetary
system via the Federal Reserve, and now the
time has come for God's End Times Word
to be Fulfilled. The Judgment Of God is
inescapable, and part of chastising a nation
of unrepentant people is by hitting them
where it hurts the most. Since so many
people have replaced God with Mammon

(Money), God will use this very same thing to bring the people of this wicked nation, and the world, to their wits end.

America will go through a period known as Hyperinflation just before the system capsizes. This is when the prices of goods and services rise considerably in a relatively short period of time. Most Americans simply will not be able to afford/survive this economic hardship. The cost of living will simply be too much for the people to bear and many millions of people will fall to the wayside and Perish during this season. I hope that you all really are taking heed to the things that I am telling you, for all of our lives are at stake and the worst part is that many people will be completely caught off guard.

I will not go into the full detail in this book on every single component of how it will happen so as to not overload you all with information. The rabbit hole goes very deep and this particular section of the book honestly requires a separate book of its own. But I do strongly recommend you all to open your eyes up before it's too late and you are caught on the wrong side of the fence. This period is simply going to separate the prepared from the unprepared; the obedient to God's commands, from the disobedient to God's commands. Wealth transfer is what will take place and many people will immediately be weeded out lose everything they have, seemingly overnight.

Chapter 4

Natural Disasters

The Bible Speaks about a number of natural disasters that are to occur during this Specific End Times period. In the Book Of Revelations, when the 6th seal is opened, a great earthquake will happen;

Revelations 6 : 12;

"And I beheld when he had opened the 6th seal, and lo, there was a great earthquake; and the sun became black as sackcloth of hair, and the moon became as blood."

Now, according to many testimonies, in which people from all over the world have been shown visions and dreams of the end times by God, there will indeed be the greatest earthquake to ever happen in the history of man. Specifically an earthquake that will just about split America in half and cause the map to have to be redrawn to fit the new "fashion" look of this "country". Other testimonies alongside this one reveal that the states of New York, California, Florida, and Puerto Rico will be destroyed by God in ONE HOUR. New York, Florida, and most of the Eastern Coast will be wiped out by a Tsunami. California will be destroyed by an Earthquake. Puerto Rico will also practically be wiped out entirely.

As I'm sure you can imagine, this is an extremely serious event that is to transpire. These are the Judgments of God that we are talking about here. A nation such as America which has been long over due for Judgment/Chastisement. An Unrepentant nation that has rejected God and Blasphemed His Holy Name for such a long period of time. I would consider these fairly light punishments. Especially considering the many other Judgments that are to befall this wicked nation.

Millions of people will perish from these natural disasters alone, and we still have yet to even get to the second half of the Great Tribulation, and that's assuming that these Natural Disasters could even be considered a part of the first half of it. Please Dear people take heed or at least CONSIDER what I'm revealing to you all here.

I'm sure that there will be a number of other natural disasters happening in other places around the world, but I'm highlighting America because for the most part, God has allowed this nation to run its course "Scott-Free" for quite some time now. God has been EXTREMELY patient and merciful to this place. He really wants the people of the world to repent and Give their Lives to Him 100%. For It is not His Will that any man would perish in these Tragic Circumstances but Dear Readers you must Understand that at some point Chastisements must be rendered unto the Disobedient and hard hearted people. He Wants us in His Eternal Kingdom with Him, not in Hell where there is no peace or rest.

Another Biblical natural disaster is also mentioned in Revelations, when the third Angel sounded the Trumpet; a meteor named Wormwood hits the earth; Revelation 8 : 10 - 11:

10."And the third angel sounded, and there fell a great star from heaven, burning as it were a lamp, and it fell upon the third part of the rivers, and upon the fountains of

waters."

11. And the name of the star is called

Wormwood: and the third part of the waters

became wormwood; and many men died of

the waters, because they were made bitter."

These scriptures tell us that a Meteor

named Wormwood is going to collide with

earth and cover 33.3% of the water that is on

it. This water will then be likened unto the

substances that is on the Meteor, thus killing

many people. For a number of years now

there have been several incidents in which

meteors flew close to/past earth, and even a

case in which some landed, although they

were very small in stature. But obviously

this one will be much larger, given the fact

that it will COVER 33% Of the water on the

Earth when it lands.

Chapter 5

World War III

The Book Of Daniel and Ezekiel reveals to us certain details about WWIII. In Chapter 7 of Daniel, the Lord gave him a Vision of 4 Beasts.

Daniel 1 : 3 – 7 ; 3. "And four great beasts came up from the sea, diverse one from the other.

4. The first was like a lion, and had eagle's wings: I beheld till the wings thereof were plucked, and it was lifted up from the earth, and made stand upon the feet as a man, and a man's heart was given unto it.

***The first beast was basically a Lion which also had the Ability to Fly, "eagle's wings"; those wings represent America and Europe, which have been allies for a very long period of time. It's "wings were plucked"; this means that these countries, which have acted and roamed the earth as Lions and Eagles means that they will collapse. The scripture didn't say that the beast altogether was destroyed, but it's very advantageous ability to "fly", was taken away (plucked). Those 2 nations, particularly America has "dominated" the economic arena for quite some time – mainly after the second world war when the US Dollar became the Reserve Currency of the World. Now is the season for God's Judgment to come upon this nation, and its Federal Reserve System with its Petrodollar scheme.

5. And behold another beast, a second, like to a bear, and it raised up itself on one side, and it had three ribs in the mouth of it between the teeth of it: and they said thus

unto it, Arise, devour much flesh.

***The bear represents the country of Russia. The three ribs in its mouth represent the nations in which they will War against and defeat. The bear was told to "Arise", and devour much flesh; it was given the command to go and war against the other Nations. Russia will be accompanied by its allies such as Syria, Iran, Cuba, China, etc. America, Lion with Eagle's Wings, will be invaded from the East and West Coast, alongside the southern states, by the Bear and its allies.

6. After this I beheld, and lo another, like a leopard, which had upon the back of it four wings of a fowl; the beast had also four heads; and dominion was given to it.

***This beast represents the country of China. The fact that it's a leopard reveals how clever the Chinese people have been in their dealings with the rest of the world, particularly America. The four heads represent the rest of the BRICS Nations; Brazil, Russia, India, and South Africa. China has load up on US debt, and are now at this moment moving away from the very corrupted US Dollar system. These nations are the rising economic markets in the world, as the age old western empires crumble.

This scripture also tells us that dominion was given unto it. Shortly thereafter the demise of America's economy, China, the up and coming "financiers" in the World Economy, will have dominion, although it will be very short lived. These partner nations are establishing institutions that will allow them more freedoms to operate outside of the US Dollar/Petro-Dollar system. The Asian Infrastructure Investment Bank, The New Development Bank with its Contingency Reserve Agreement; these institutions will allow the partnering countries to be in a better position to propel their country forward. These institutions were established partly because one of the current world banking establishments, International \ Monetary Fund, dominated by the United States, refuses to pass the 2010 Reforms which would give the rising economies a greater share of voting power; which is only a very small amount.

7. After this I saw in the night visions, and behold a fourth beast, dreadful and terrible, and strong exceedingly; and it had great iron teeth: it devoured and brake in pieces, and

stamped the residue with the feet of it: and it was diverse from all the beasts that were before it; and it had ten horns.

***This beast represents the Antichrist which will come after World War III and the Global Economic Collapse. The ten horns represent 10 kingdoms around the world which will be under the Antichrist's dominion. "It devoured and brake in pieces, and stamped the residue with feet of it", tells us that the Antichrist will be very tyrannical and evil. He will be the head of the New World Order as they carry out their global depopulation agenda under his orders. The fact that this beast was more diverse from the others shows us that his ways and thoughts, demeanor and charisma was far more apparent and attractive than the other beasts before him.

In the following Chapter, 8, God gave Daniel another vision, of a ram and a he goat:

"3. Then I lifted up mine eyes, and saw, and behold, there stood before the river a ram which had two horns: and the two horns were high; but one was higher than the other, and the higher came up last.

***The two horns on the Ram represent America and Europe. These nations have been allies via the corrupt Banking families; not only this but their pushing in these different directions represents them gaining territory, influence, and dominion over other nations in the world. The US has also been a dominant military power in the world for a lengthy season. Through various methodologies they have defeated and subtly overthrown other smaller nations over the past several years. The Petro-Dollar has also played a major role in America becoming a dominant economic power in the world.

4. I saw the ram pushing westwards, and northward, and southward; so that no beast might stand before him, neither was there any that could deliver out of his hand; but he did according to his will, and became great.

5. And as I was considering, behold, a he goat came from the west on the face of the whole earth, and touched not the ground: and the goat had a notable horn between his eyes.

6. And he came to the Ram that had two horns, which I had seen standing before the river, and ran unto him in the fury of his power.

7. And I saw him come close unto the Ram, and he was moved with Choler against him, and smote the Ram, and brake his two horns: and there was no power in the ram to stand before him, but he cast him down to the ground, and stamped upon him: and there was none that could deliver the Ram out of his hand.

8. Therefore the he goat waxed very great: and when he was strong, the great horn was broken; and for it came up four notable ones toward the four winds of Heaven.

***The "he goat" mentioned in verse 5 is Russia. These past 3 scriptures tell us that Russia, the "he goat", will invade and destroy both America and Europe. It is those 2 countries that keep placing Economic sanctions on Russia in attempt to hurt its economy. The odd thing about that is the fact that Russia's economy is in far better shape than America and Europe to be able to withstand economic attacks. But even still, everyone has their limits, we can only take so much before we retaliate, and since we know that God is Sovereignand holds the hearts of the Kings of the Earth in His Hands, we know that soon, God Will turn the Heart of Russia's leader to Chastise those two nations.

Many people will perish at the hands of Russia and its allies. It will not matter if you're in auniform or not. We also must remember that all of the world's leaders, although they may have minor "differences" with each other, work for the same people. They are ultimately not the decision makers in this global circumstance. So here we have again – millions upon millions of men, women, and children alike will lose their lives in yet another well thought out, meticulously orchestrated war.

But in seeing this with Spiritual eyes you will see that it is a just Judgment for the nations of the World whom have been Un-Repentant and live instead a lifestyle of Sin and Iniquity. This has been the case all throughout history; wicked men see wars as a way of substantial Profits at the cost of human lives; God sees Wars as a way to Chastise Rebellious people. So he allows Spiritual Wickedness in high places to foment these wars via fleshly human pawns on the earth who know not what they do or who they truly serve. And all of this evil they conspire will come upon their own heads. Especially given the fact that they are leaders in the world, whom are entrusted with leading the people in their respective nations.

9. And out of one of them came forth a little horn, which waxed exceeding great, toward the south, and toward the east, and toward the pleasant land."

This scripture describes the Antichrist and how he will indeed rule the entire world for a short season. He will come during/after World War III and declare peace in the world, but he will be filled with Evil. More details are given on him later in the next couple of sections. But for sure you can expect to know that he means none of us any good as he will be Lucifer in the flesh and practically evil incarnate. Please do not take this lightly dear people.

World War III will begin around the same time as the economic collapse of America, or shortly afterwards. If you look at what is happening today, right now, in the global financial markets, you will inevitably see the economic warfare that is transpiring between certain countries of the world.

God tells us in 1 Timothy 6 : 10 ; For the love of money is the root of all evil: which while some coveted after, they have erred from the faith, and pierced themselves through with many sorrows."

And indeed what we have today are men and women in very high places of authority who love money more than life itself and thus utilize it to oppress the people of the world. But caught up in their own foolish arrogance they do not realize that they are being used by God to play a role in fulfilling His End

Times Agenda. But sadly, they actually believe that what they are doing is the right thing to do, how Ironic. Keep these people lifted up in prayer dear Brethren, for they are in fact truly lost and has allowed this "Love of money" to consume their entire existence.

Spiritual wickedness in High Places utilizes "pawns" on the earth to fulfill Lucifer's agenda. But the awesome thing about it all, is the fact that they are all just a peace in my Father's Bigger Picture. One nation, waging economic warfare on other countries, thus causing desperate/ drastic actions to be taken, in order to defend/preserve itself. But because all of the countries are connected to each other, there will inevitably be a domino effect. Many millions of people will perish during this war as there will be no distinguishing or separation between soldier and civilian, and this will in fact be the worst, most bloodiest war in human history.

Nuclear Warfare will be the catalyst that truly extinguishes the beauty of the earth, and purges it of the sinful old world which has corrupted it for Generations. Entire cities will be wiped off the world map in moments with the press of a button. Several million human souls will Perish from this alone. Radiation is one of the most dangerous substances in the world and the heat waves upon which it will travel will absolutely eviscerate people in seconds of making contact with their bodies. There is really no way to escape a nuclear attack unless you are living in some deep

underground bunker, and even still, your
survival isn't guaranteed.

Chapter 6

CERN

CERN, located in Switzerland, was founded in 1954, and is a European Based Nuclear Research Organization. They believe in the parallel universes theory, which basically means there are 'other' worlds on the other side of a certain "doorway". They use the largest and most expensive scientific equipment in the world to test the laws of nature. Beyond that 'public' description of what they are doing, is a much more darker and sinister function. Their main purpose is to open up a doorway into this "parallel world".

This is actually the Spirit World, in which them opening that doorway, is a huge danger to humanity and is prophesied in the Bible, The Book Of Revelations. At the headquarters of CERN, is a statue of the Hindu Goddess Shiva, which is the god Of Destruction. She is one of the triad gods of Hinduism; Shiva(Destroyer), Brahma(Creation), and Vishnu (Preservation). At CERN, they are using what is called the Large Hadron Collider, which is one of those large scientific pieces of equipment being used.

It is 300 feet underground, 17 miles long, formed in the shape of a circle and is a particle accelerating machine. Particle acceleration, as in colliding protons together inside of this machine at speeds of up to the speed of light or more. Upon collision these scientists are hoping to open the doorway to another dimension. This is very high level sorcery, a type of spirit science. Be that as it may, CERN does a play a fairly intricate role in society.

Make no mistake about it, this is another satanic institution, which, obviously, God has allowed to play a major role in how the world functions. Not to say that every person that works there is a Satan worshipper, but most certainly at the higher levels there is an undeniably evil agenda. CERN, through their employee Tim Burners Lee, the World Wide Web was created. To which, going deeper; our letter W, the 23rd letter of the Alphabet, has the Hebrew equivalent of the letter "Vav", which has a numerical value of 6. So through transliteration, you go from "www", to "666".

In the Book Of Revelations, Chapter 9, God tells us that the gate to the bottom less pit will be opened, and an army of locusts will come and torment all the people of the earth that do not have the seal of God in their foreheads, for a season of 5 months. This will obviously be a very perilous time for humanity, as will be more detailed later. Alongside these things, CERN was built at Saint-Genis Pouilly, which, in Ancient days, it was called "Apolliacum". Back in those times it was literally a temple to the false god Apollo. They believed that it was a gateway to the underworld. And in the Bible, the King of the army of locusts is named "Apollyon".

Clearly you all must be able to see the connections here. When that time comes you can only pray that you are shielded from these things, for many people will suffer terrible fates, as God tells us verbatimly in His Word, and He has placed the wicked leadership in place to carry out these things. These people are actually doing these things; this isn't some far into the future speculation being spoken on here, this stuff has been, and continues to take place in our world, at that place. The perpetrators of this evil do not know what they are truly getting their selves into. They have firmly crossed the line that us humans have no business crossing.

Chapter 7

The Rapture

There is much "disputation" amongst the Brethren In Christ in regards to this topic. There are Three viewpoints of the Rapture : Pre- Tribulation, Mid-Tribulation, and Post-Tribulation. I personally don't understand how there could be such division amongst the Body Of Christ in regards to this when the Word Of God seems to (in my eyes) spell out which one is correct. This is a very serious topic that needs to be understood by those of us in the Body Of Christ; for it could mean the difference between you being Left Behind or being caught up in the Spirit to meet the Lord Jesus Christ in the air. The last thing you want to do is get Left Behind and have to endure the Persecution Of the Antichrist.

*Pre-Tribulation : This viewpoint holds that Jesus will Rapture the Church and the Antichrist will rule the World via The New World Order for 7 years. This 7 year period will begin when the Peace Treaty with Israel is declared. The 7 year period is known as The Great Tribulation. I don't have much input on this viewpoint other than the fact that it's simply not scriptural at all; but I do indeed understand how/why it could be mis-interpreted.

*Mid-Tribulation : This viewpoint holds that Jesus will Rapture the Church after The Great Tribulation has already began. After as in, the Mark of Beast has been mandated, or somewhere around the 3 and a half year period of the 7 year Peace Treaty with Israel. Jesus states pretty clearly in Matthew

24 : 21 – 22 that Mid-Trib is indeed the case. 21 : "For then shall there be Great Tribulation, such as was not since the beginning of the world to this time, no, nor ever shall be." 22 : "And except those days should be shortened, there should no flesh be saved: but for the elect's Sake those days shall be shortened." ; God is telling us here that He will, for the sake of His elect, shorten the days here on Earth, as if to say that its going to get SO bad, that if He doesn't shorten the days, even His elect wouldn't be Saved.

This shortening of the days happens during the Great Tribulation period, as in, when the 3 and hald year period is done, then the Lord will return for Judgment day and establishment of New Jerusalem. If that was not the case, then Jesus would have said nothing at all about those days being cut short for our sake. Those scriptures concern the overall scope of the nature of the Great Tribulation period and how/why God will shorten the days; the next scriptures show the definite confirmation that His believers specifically will not be here on earth the entire time of the Great Tribulation.

Revelations 7 : 9 – 14 and 2nd Thessalonians confirms the Mid-Tribulation Rapture : God was giving John a vision of the End Of Time, and what would happen unto His people during that season Of Great Tribulation – this vision came immediately after God had showed him the vision of the 144,000 thousand, bloodline Israelites who had been sealed to be protected during the reign of the Antichrist.

Revelations 7 : 9; "After this I beheld, and lo, a great multitude, which no man could number, of all nations, and kindreds, and people, and tongues, stood before the throne, and before the Lamb, clothed with white robes, and palms in their hands;

10. And cried with a loud voice, saying Salvation to our God, which Sitteth upon the throne, and unto the Lamb.

11. And all the angels stood round about the throne, and about the elders and the four beasts, and fell before the throne on their faces, and worshipped God,

12. Saying, Amen: Blessing, and glory, and wisdom, and thanksgiving, and honor, and power, and might, be unto our God for ever and ever. Amen.

13. And one of the elders answered, saying unto me, What are these which are arrayed in white robes? And whence came they?

14. And I said unto him, Sir, thou Knowest. And he said to me, These are they which CAME OUT of Great Tribulation, and have washed their robes, and made them white in the blood of the Lamb."

This scripture clearly tells us that a Great Multitude, from all nations, and kindreds, and people, and tongues, will be taken out (Raptured) DURING the Great Tribulation period. The fact that the scripture specifically says "came out of Great Tribulation", tells us 1.) Great Tribulation was already happening on the earth; and 2.) Only the Purified Christians whom have had their Hearts Cleansed through Jesus Christ will be Raptured.

These are the Christians whom Live their Entire Lives according to God's Word. They are not Lukewarm and do not Commit Iniquity. They have truly had their Hearts and Minds Transformed by God.

*Post-Tribulation : This viewpoint holds that the Rapture and the 2nd Return Of Jesus Christ are one and the same, and that there will be no "secret Rapture" of the Church before that time. The believers of this viewpoint also like to quote from the very same chapter of Matthew, but a few scriptures later – 29 : "Immediately after the tribulation of those days shall the sun be darkened, and the moon shall not give her light, and the stars shall fall from heaven, and the powers of the heavens shall be shaken:" They also put emphasis on the "after the tribulation" part of that scripture;

but they tend to not realize that the Rapture and the 2nd coming are two separate events, otherwise it would make no sense what so ever for Jesus to have said anything about the Elect's days being "shortened" in verse 22. If there is no Rapture at all before OR During the Great Tribulation, what sense does it make for Jesus to say anything about our days being "shortened"? And for our days to be "shortened" can ONLY imply that those who rejected Jesus or committed Iniquity will continue to be here on earth to endure the rest of the Great Tribulation, until scriptures 29 – 31 come to pass, which is at the end of the Great Tribulation period.

Chapter 8

The Hour Of Temptation

The Hour of Temptation, as described in Revelations 3 : 10 ; "Because thou hast kept the word of my patience, I also will keep thee from the hour of temptation, which shall come upon all the world, to try them that dwell upon the earth."This "temptation" is the final false flag move against humanity before the Mark of The Beast is mandated. It is the Elite's last attempt to fleece the people of the world into falling for what they desire. This Deception will be centered around the lie of an "Alien" deception. Due to several generations of mass conditioning and indoctrination, most people are going to fall for it. I guess you can say that the leaders of this world are pulling out all of the stops for this one, as they are desperate for us to fall into their hands and accept "their" New World Order system.

While we live life on the run and in caves and in FEMA camps, they continue to live life "lavishly" in their undergrounds cities, but oh no, God has quite a surprise for them! The Elite have successfully convinced the world that there exists a fairy tale location called "Outer Space", and that the earth is a spinning globe in this place, rotating around the Sun, and that the Sun is in the center of these other planets, including the Earth, which are all rotating around the sun at thousands of miles per hour. And with this, that there are other thousands of Galaxies in the far reaches of this place called "Outer Space", and that there "may be", or "is" "other" life forms in existence in these places. I'm sure you've all heard of the "mysterious" place called "Area 51", and the various "Alien" encounters which have happened in the past. These disclosures are nothing more than propaganda and subtle conditioning for the sleeping masses to be ready for the ultimate test of mankind.

"Aliens" are actually Fallen Angels in disguise. As I mentioned earlier in the book, and as God tells us in the Bible, we wrestle not against Flesh and Blood, but against Spiritual wickedness in high places; those are literally the entities in which God was referring to, the beings which He kicked out of His Kingdom. It is these beings which "control" the world we live in today through the Luciferian Elite families of the world. The Grand Deception itself will be an "Alien Invasion" of Earth. Intergalactic

species will come and take over our world
and be our "New" leaders.

They will have traveled far and long
across the far reaches of "outer space" to
conquer and dominate us, and or in tandem
with CERN, having opened a gateway to
hell itself through their sorcery induced
scientific practices. Because people are
ALREADY so brainwashed into believing
the lies of leaders concerning our planet, as
in, people believe the Earth is a giant
spinning basketball around the sun
in outer space, they will easily fall for this.
What's even more sad is that when you try
and tell people about how the earth is
actually flat and enclosed in a dome, they
will laugh, mock, and ridicule you as if
you're crazy, but in "our" world, that's
nothing new, just another day in the life of

someone that spreads the truth in dying world. This deception will usher in the Great Tribulation and the Reign of the Antichrist. which are detailed in the following sections.

Do not be deceived dear people; again I say, Aliens are Fallen Angels, SPIRITUAL beings whom will have taken on physical bodies and will now then live amongst us and aid in the depopulating of human kind. Project Blue Beam also can/ will/most likely will play another large role in this Hour Of Deception. The scripture tells us that this temptation will come upon all humanity, as in we all will be tested at the same time. Correlate this to Revelations 13, where God is describing the Antichrist and False Prophet; verses 13 and 14, 13 : "And he doeth great wonders so that he maketh fire come down from heaven on the earth in the sight of men….

14. And deceiveth them that dwell on the earth by the means of those miracles which he had power to do in the sight of the beast; saying to them that dwell on the earth, that they should make an image to the beast, which had the wound by a sword, and did live." These scriptures are telling us that the Antichrist and False prophet will have the ability to deceive the people of the world, and emphasis is placed on the "by the means" part of verse 14. Project Blue Beam is a highly advanced hologram projection type operation, they are able to do some stunning things with that technology. Just do a Google search on these things for yourselves what I'm talking about.

Please be prayed up on these things dear people. Keep in mind that MOST people are going to fall for this grand deception! They rejected these truths that we revealed to them for all these years, therefore God will give their mind over into the hands of the enemy when he pulls this final trick. Project Blue Beam, mixed with CERN operations of portal/gateway opening and we have ourselves quite the theatrical show before ourselves. Another thing to note is the "Scientific Research" being conducted down in Antarctica, to which no one is allowed there except it be by special, guided voyages.

Chapter 9

The Great Tribulation

This period in History begins in Chapter 6 of Revelations. Each horse is a metaphorical depiction of what will transpire during this time. The first half of the Great Tribulation (3 and half years), will be the timeframe of these horsemen coming to pass. If you align what each of them represent, to what is happening in the world today, and what will be happening, you will indeed see that we are in perfect alignment with Biblical Prophecies; specifically The Horsemen, who began the Judgments from God in the beginning of Chapter 6. I will only expand on the six seals here, and leave the rest for another release.

Other parts of Revelations are mentioned elsewhere in this book. In verse 2 of that Chapter, One of the four beasts revealed to John "a white horse: and he that sat on him had a bow; and a crown was given unto him: and he went forth conquering, and to conquer.

***This horseman represents a religious and political power that will conquer the world during this time. Many nations will be subject to this agenda unfolding. The Religious power represents the nation of Islam that is rapidly gaining Dominion in the World, via other parties involved. Islam will eventually be the "heavy handed" dominating spiritual force during this time in which the Antichrist will use forcibly. The Political Power represents the "Elite" and their "pawns" whom preside in several, various regions of the earth, setting up and establishing "their" agenda.

4. And there went out another horse that was red: and power was given to him that sat thereon to take peace from the earth, and that they should kill one another: and there was given unto him a great sword.

***This horse represents World War III and the social meltdown that will be happening around the world during this period. Peace being taken from the earth can only imply that the people of the world will be turned against one another. As we see, and as few of us discern, Racism continues to thrive and it is being used by elite powers to divide the people up and to bring the world and specifically America into yet another civil war. "And that they should kill one another:

and there was given unto him a great "sword.", this part of the scripture tells us exactly what the people will be doing.

I have a separate section just for WWIII due to the magnitude of it. But just know that outside of how catastrophic that event will be itself, the domestic violence that will transpire throughout our communities during this season will be very bad. Not only that, but the rate/timeframe in which these things are going to be happening is upon us and unfolding right before our eyes. Armed militias will/are forming at this moment in hopes to protect their lives and their loved ones; or to fulfill to some misguided sense of "Patriotism". It is a very unwise thing to do and these militias are laughably outmanned and outgunned without a question.

5. And when he had opened the third seal, I heard the third beast say, Come and see. And I beheld, and lo a black horse; and he that sat on him had a pair of balances in his hand.

6. And I heard a voice in the midst of the four beasts say, A measure of wheat for a penny, and three measures of barley for a penny; and see thou hurt not the oil and the wine.

***This seal represents economic hardship. America is the most indebted nation in the world and is only getting worse. People seem to believe that everything is alright or is going to get better, which is completely not the case at all. There is period known as "Hyperinflation", which is what is being described in these scriptures. "A measure of wheat for a penny, and three measures of barley for a penny;", gives an exact replica of what the prices of goods and services will be like during these times. People simply will not be able to afford to survive.

7. And when he had the fourth seal, I heard the voice of the fourth beast say, Come and see.

8. And I looked, and behold a pale horse: and his name that sat on him was Death, and Hell followed with him. And power was given unto them over the fourth part of the earth, to kill with the sword, and with hunger, and with death, and with the beasts of the earth.

The fourth seal describes a scene of absolute sorrow and desperation. This is the time in which around 2 billion people will be depopulated from the planet. The enforcement of the laws and regulations will be brutal as the people will be under heavy oppression from the civil authorities. The hunger pains will come from people not being able to afford to eat as the cost of living will have risen far out of most people's reach. The beasts of the earth is still a little blurry to me in terms of how that will actually pan out; but it would seem as though it can be taken literal.

Dreadful times will be upon the people of the world as most of them will be rounded up and taken off to modern day concentration camps (FEMA Camps). There are several hundred of these camps all over America so I can only imagine how many "similar" camps there are all over the world. Martial law will be in full effect as the police force is being heavily militarized and risen to the next level of capability. Society as we know it will fall completely apart and there will be anarchy in the streets. Disease will plague the people as another form of chastisement for disobedience. Although these "plagues" are usually laboratory experiments which have been injected into someone/something and spread throughout the general populace. The Plague itself is going to kill many millions of people.

9. And when he had opened the fifth seal, I saw under the altar the souls of them that were slain for the word of God, and for the testimony which they held:

10. And they cried with a loud voice, saying, How long, O Lord, holy and true, dost thou not Judge and avenge our blood on them that dwell on the earth?

11. And white robes were given unto every one of them; and it was said unto them, that

they should rest yet for a little season, until their fellow servants also and their brethren, that should be killed as they were, should be fulfilled.

This seal describes the martyrdom of Christians during this time. Jesus told us specifically in Matthew 24 that we would be hated of all men for His Name's Sake. This implies that we will be full time/entirely under the Antichrist New World Order system. Christians have been Martyred since the beginning of Christianity, but this season of Persecution will be far worse than any of the others. As we are seeing now, Christians are at this moment in time being killed in horrific manners in various parts of the world for their Faith.

They are being killed by followers of Islam; terrorist groups who are devoted to carrying out the direct and specific orders from their god Allah. Islam is the Rod that the Antichrist will use to oppress and kill people that do not follow his agenda. This religious belief is being propagated to the masses and they have been for some time now gaining much support and political clout to further "their" agenda. Christians here in America for the most part have no idea what's coming as they are being fed a whole heap of ear tickling sermons that only serve to keep them comfortable in their cozy lifestyle.

But not only will there be people from the religion of Islam killing Christians; it will also be "normal" everyday citizens who have been brainwashed by the

Antichrist into believing that Christians are terrorists. God will have given them over to reprobate minds therefore anyone who does not completely follow Jesus Christ will be subject to the devices/deceptions of the enemy, as they already are for the most part. Christians will be hunted down like wild animals during this time and treated will evil intent. Many Brethren in Christ will fall away and reject Jesus during this time as it will simply be too much for them to bare. We will live in the wilderness, caves, underground, etc during this time.

12. And I beheld when he had opened the sixth seal, and, lo, there was a great earthquake; and the sun became black as sackcloth of hair, and the moon became as blood;

13. And the stars of heaven fell unto the earth, even as a fig tree casteth her untimely figs, when she is shaken of a mighty wind.

14. And the heaven departed as a scroll when it is rolled together; and every mountain and island were moved out of their places.

Throughout the Bible, God tells us that a Blood Moon will be the notable sign of His return. There is also a separate section on the Blood Moons. The earthquake described here in scripture will perhaps be the biggest to ever strike the world. Testimonies from people who have been shown this earthquake from God describe it as one that will tear America in half, literally. This earthquake is described more in a separate section but the scriptures following it paints a picture of everyone being afraid, supposing that Jesus has returned in the midst of it.

The Great Tribulation will be the worse time period in human history. As Jesus Himself said in Matthew 24 : 21; "For then shall be great tribulation, such as was not since the beginning of the world to this time, no, nor ever shall be. Many people have "heard" about this or are "familiar" with it, but very few have the slightest clue as to just how serious it will be. This is the period in which The Book Of Revelations and The New World Order Agenda will really be accelerated and fully manifested. Alongside this, it's the period in which most of the human population will be exterminated with Extreme Prejudice.

This period will begin when the
Antichrist breaks the 7 year peace treaty
with Israel. For those who have the eyes to
see, they will immediately know that this is
the time to flee towards a faraway place.
People have refused to Repent and give their
lives to Jesus Christ therefore God will give
them over to Reprobate minds and allow
them to be deceived by the Enemy on all
fronts. Even some of the professing
Christians will fall prey to the deceptions
that are to befall this world, thus free
handedly giving their hearts and minds over
to the Antichrist during this time and
forfeiting their free gift of eternal life and
choosing instead to perish in the lake of fire.

The Bible gives specific numerical
accountability of just how many people will
die during this time. Now, if we look at

whom God is using, to fulfill His Perfect Will, you will see, that "their" agenda is to reduce the population to 500 million people. Now, let's assume that there are 7.5 Billion people in the world when this specific time of Great Tribulation begins. The Book Of Revelations States in Chapter 9 : 15 ; "And the four angels were loosed, which were prepared for an hour, and a day, and a month, and a year, for to slay the third part of men.".......

That is one third of the entire global population, or 33.3% people, or 2.5 Billion people. Who are the four angels that carried this out? Hmmmm.... Right after this are the horsemen, who slay another 3rd of the human population, 2.5 Billion people; that's 5 Billion people perished. Who are the horsemen? Those are Soldiers, most likely

United Nations Soldiers. And where do the other 2 Billion come from? These are mentioned in Revelations 6 : 8 ; "And I looked, and behold a pale horse: and his name that sat on him was Death, and Hell followed him. And power was given unto them over the fourth part of the earth, to kill with the sword, and with hunger, and with death, and with the beasts of the earth." That fourth part of the earth is 25% of the human population, or 1.87 Billion(exact) People. If you do the math, that's right around 7 Billion people, which leaves around 500 million people left. This falls just about perfectly in line with Satan's New World Order agenda – how so? Because God is USING the leaders of this "New World Order" To carry out HIS plan. But these wicked and evil men actually believe that they are doing ALL OF THIS EVIL in their own "human" Wisdom, following after Satan.

For those of you that STILL don't believe in this after ALL of this being presented here, Here are a few quotes from very powerful, evil men who have worked behind the scenes at some point in history, or currently today, that have PUBLICLY promoted or gloated about this "agenda" of "theirs":"We are not going to achieve a New World Order without paying for it in blood as well as in words and money."
- Arthur Schlesinger Jr., 'The CFR Journal Foreign Affairs', August 1975.

"No one will enter the New World Order unless he or she will make a pledge to worship Lucifer. No one will enter the New

Age unless he will take a Luciferian

Initiation."

David Spangler, Director of Planetary
Initiative, United Nations

"We shall have world government whether

or not you like it, by conquest or consent."

Statement by Council on Foreign Relations

(CFR) member James Warburg to The

Senate Foreign Relations Committee on

February 17th, 1950

These men are not even realizing that
they are promoting God's Word to come to
pass. There are numerous more quotes from
various other individuals that validate this,
so if you STILL are "skeptical" then I can
only conclude that you simply do not want
to believe. I pray that you awaken before it's

too late and receive Salvation from the Lord Jesus Christ. He is the only way to escape the worse of these things, specifically that being eternal hellfire. Sadly, most, if not all of the men and women who say such things as mentioned above actually want to go to hell, foolishly believing that they will be rewarded when they get there, not grasping the fact that they too will burn in hell for all eternity alongside Lucifer and the rest of the fallen angels.

Chapter 10

The Antichrist

The Antichrist is described in detail in the Bible. If you look at the current Political Roster of people in the world today, and allow God to guide you into the truth, you will know who he is. In Daniel, Chapter 7, and Revelations, Chapter 13, God describes to us who the Antichrist and False Prophet are, which will lead and deceive the whole world away from God. It will be Lucifer, the leader of the Fallen Angels from God's Heavenly Kingdom, whom Inhabit the Heart and Mind and manipulate the human vessel here on Earth. The False Prophet, as the title itself implies, is a religious figure who will serve as "2nd in command" during the Antichrist's reign.

1. And I stood upon the sand of the sea, and saw a beast rise up out of the sea, having seven heads and ten horns, and upon his horns ten crowns, and upon his heads the name of blasphemy.

***The seven heads represent the 7 kings of the earth and the 10 crowns represent 10 kingdoms. The Antichrist will have dominion over all of these of the Earth during this time. Revelations 13 : 2 ; "And the beast which I saw was like unto a leopard, and his feet were as the feet of a bear, and his mouth as the mouth of a lion: and the dragon gave him his power, and his seat, and great authority."

***This is a description of the Antichrist.
These animal features come right from the
vision which was shown to Daniel, of the
four beats.

"The dragon gave him his power, and his
seat, and great authority", is telling us that it
is Lucifer that will give the human on earth
his official "Antichrist" title. Again,
discernment of the Holy Spirit will guide
you into all truths.

2. And I saw one of his heads as it were

   wounded to death; and his deadly

   wound was healed: and all the world

   wondered after the beast.

***This scripture describes to us the actual
scene, that will come to pass here on earth,
which will alert us to when the Antichrist's

time has officially began. His deadly wound can only come from 1 of 3 sources; accident, assassination attempt, false flag attack. Either way, shortly thereafter his wound will be healed; either by laying on of hands from some high ranking religious figure, or just another part to a grander deception against the masses. And of course, an event of this magnitude with this type of outcome would have a huge impact on those who are not awake.

3. And they worshipped the dragon which gave power to the beast: and they worshipped the beast, saying, Who is like unto the beast? Who is able to make war with him?

***Here we are being told that the people will so given to the satanic system, after being taken astray by the deadly wound, that they are going to worship the devil himself, and the Antichrist.

They will defend him, reverence him, follow his every order (or be executed).

4. And there was given unto him a mouth speaking great things and blasphemies; and power was given unto him to continue forty and two months.

***The Antichrist will be very foul mouthed against God and the Body Of Christ. He will "Blasphemy" God and speak extensively proud in his attitude. He will also be given power "TO CONTINUE" forty and two months. "To Continue" tells us that he had already been in power – he was given an "extended" period of time to have his authority. Forty and two months is 3 and a half years, which is the 2nd half of the Great Tribulation period. Revelations 13 :

6. "And he opened his mouth in blasphemy against God, to blaspheme his name, and his tabernacle, and them that dwell in heaven.

7. And it was given unto him to make war with the saints, and to overcome them: and power was given him over all kindreds, and tongues, and nations.

8. And all that dwell upon the earth shall worship him, whose names are not written in the book of Life of the Lamb slain from the foundation of the world.

9. If any man have an ear, let him hear.

10. He that leadeth into captivity shall go into captivity: he that killeth with the sword must be killed with the sword. Here is the patience and the faith of the saints."

*** These scriptures tell us that not only will the Antichrist blaspheme the Body Of Christ, but he will war against it/Christians. We are also told that he will overcome us and have dominion over the entire world. Everyone who's name isn't written in the Book Of Life will worship him. It is during this period that the people who reject him, will live their lives on the run, which is described in verse 10. The saints of God will truly be tested like never before during this time.

Everyone who does not worship the image of the beast/Antichrist will be put to death, as spoken in Revelations 13 : 15; "And he had power to give life unto the image of the beast, that the image of the beast should both speak, and cause that as many as would not worship the image of the beast should be killed." Billions of people will perish during this season of Global Persecution, especially the Christians. The image of the Beast will be created via a long term construct in the making named "Project Blue Beam", as mentioned in Revelations 13 : 14; "And deceiveth them that dwell on the earth BY THE MEANS of those miracles which he had power to do in the sight of the beast; saying to them that dwell on the earth, that they should make an image to the beast, which had the wound by a sword, and did live."

"By the means" that is spoken of in the scripture above is telling us there is a specific method/process/technology that will allow the 2nd Beast to carry out these

deceptions. I will not go into detail here as
to what Project Blue Beam is so I encourage
you all to do your due diligence so that you
can get a very clear understanding as to what
it is and what role it has played and will play
in the coming time(s). Most people will be
as they are today, completely deceived and
living in a world of absolute disillusionment.
As sad as this is, this is simply the world
that we live in. People would much rather sit
around and watch TV all day than
make the necessary changes to their lives
that would solidify their position in the
Kingdom Of Heaven.

Who is the Antichrist? I will not
state his name here, but I strongly urge you
all to ask the Lord to lead you to the answer.
But I will tell you that he is in fact in power
right now. All of you have most certainly

seen or heard of him before. God will indeed allow this man to persecute the entire world and trample it under foot at his will.

Most people will die horrible deaths and be forced to undergo brutal suffering and punishment. Honestly, words will never be able to describe the level at which this is going to occur; search your hearts right now dear people; allow the Lord God, Jesus Christ into your lives so that you may be counted worthy to inherit His Eternal Kingdom.

All of you whose names are not written in God's Book of Life will bow down and be forced to accept the Mark Of The Beast. You will worship and reverence him day and night or be executed or tortured beyond what you could ever possibly imagine. Or you will have to live your life in captivity for the rest of your days until it's all over with. From this point many people will starve to death or resort to cannibalizing each other for survival, since they will not be able to buy or sell anything unless they have his Mark. And when I say captivity, I mean that you will be living in mountains, caves, forests, wooded locations, underground, etc.

You simply will have no other choice of survival. If you remain in the cities and try to survive, it will only be a matter of time before you are captured or killed by the "Police/military" forces. The police will be Judge, Jury, and Executioner on the spot. It will be at their sole discretion as to rather or not you will live if they capture you without the Mark Of The Beast. But in most cases, they will in fact choose to execute you.

You think police brutality is bad now? Just wait until all of THIS begins to come to pass. Dear readers, I implore you to Understand the Magnitude of these Circumstances, and to also Know and internalize the Fact that it is not my Father's Will that you Perish, without first Knowing His Son Jesus Christ as your Lord And Savior.

For the Brethren In Christ whom are Left Behind; you must be strong in the Faith. If you are captured by the Enemy, it is critical that you are able to endure whatever pain and suffering the Antichrist puts you through. That very short period of time of suffering will be nothing compared to the Eternal Glory that you are to inherit in God's Eternal Kingdom. That is assuming you have purified your hearts and are no longer operating in Iniquity. Many of the Brethren In Christ Will Renounce Jesus under the immense pressure and will snap like a twig as if they never knew Jesus during this time.

Many of my fellow Brethren are very "gung ho" about being Martyred for Jesus. Although this is a very valiant and honorable thing, perhaps one of the highest honors, it is critical that you are HUMBLE and that you PRAY for the STRENGTH to endure. Being Martyred is not some cake walk dear Brethren. Yes, there are already 10s of thousands of Guillotines awaiting us who believe; but take serious note Brethren; if you are chosen to be Beheaded, you are seriously blessed. To elaborate on this I mean that you could have easily been chosen to undergo days of horrifying torture instead, which would yield an exponentially higher chance of you rejecting Jesus and accepting the Mark Of The Beast.

And Of Course, God tells us in Revelations that all of those who accept The Mark Of The Beast will burn and spend an Eternity separated from God in The Lake of Fire. God does not want this for you dear people but it is the inevitable and only outcome for all of those who reject His Free Gift of Salvation through His Only Begotten Son Jesus Christ. Your money, fame, power, authority, popularity, intellect, etc, are completely irrelevant and will not matter one inch when it is all said and done. God is not a respecter of persons therefore everyone will be on equal standing and Judged righteously according to His Holy Word. There is no other way around this dear people so I truly hope that you decide right now at this moment where you want to spend eternity.

Chapter 11

The Return Of Yeshua

The 2nd Coming of our Lord and Savior Jesus Christ Will be the most Glorious day in all the History of the World. Throughout Scripture, Jesus Likens His Return to that as a thief in the night. The Book of Matthew and Revelations paints a vivid picture of how the Return Of Jesus Will be. All of the naysayers, scoffers, "mockers", etc will be put to shame as the King of Heaven and Earth Will reveal Himself to the Entire World as the Judge of the Living and the Dead. Matthew 24 : 27 – 31 tells us :

"27. For as the lightning cometh out of the east, and shineth even unto the west; so shall also the coming of the Son of man be.

28. For wheresoever the carcase is, there will the eagles be gathered together.

29. Immediately after the tribulation of those days shall the sun be darkened, and the moon shall not give her light, and the stars shall fall from heaven, and the powers of the heavens shall be shaken:

30. And then shall appear the sign of the Son of man in heaven: and then shall all the tribes of the earth mourn, and they shall see the Son of man coming in the clouds of heaven with power and great glory.

31. And he shall send his angels with a great sound of a trumpet, and they shall gather together his elect from the four winds, from one end of heaven to the other."

***These scriptures describe to us the scenery that will transpire in the heavens above when He Returns. The sun being

darkened, moon with no light, powers of
heaven being shaken; the world will be
affected greatly by His Coming. The "elect"
that are being gathered from "the four
winds, from one end of heaven to the other"
are the chosen children of God, those whom
have purified their selves in the Blood Of
Jesus Christ. Previous to these particular
scriptures Jesus gave warnings/caution on
the False Christs that will come and claim to
be Him. Sadly, most people will be deceived
by these imposers of Jesus and will fall
away into an even deeper state of
disillusionment.

The Book Of Revelations also gives
a very detailed description of what will
happen on that glorious day. Revelations 19
: 11 – 21, tells us that not only is this the day
that Jesus Will Return, but it is also the day

that the Kingdoms of the World will gather to try and overcome Jesus and His Army, but they are swiftly defeated by His Sword.

> 11. And I saw Heaven opened, and behold a white horse; and he that sat upon him was called Faithful and True, and in righteousness he doth Judge and make war.

> 12. His eyes were as a flame of fire, and on his head were many crowns; and he had a name written, that no man knew, but he himself.

> 13. And he was clothed with a vesture dipped in blood: and his name is called The Word of God.

> 14. And the armies which were in heaven followed him upon white horses, clothed in fine linen, white and clean.

15. And out of his mouth goeth a sharp sword, that with it he should smite the nations: and he shall rule them with a rod of iron: and he treadeth the winepress of the fierceness and wrath of Almighty God.

16. And he hath on his vesture and on his thigh a name written, KING OF KINGS, AND LORD OF LORDS.

***Above we are given a description of Jesus' appearance, His name, and the Army that will accompany Him on that Great Day. He will be the King, the Ruler, and the Judge, of the New Jerusalem, The Kingdom Of God.

17. And I saw an angel standing in the sun; and he cried with a loud voice, saying to all the fowls that fly in the midst of heaven, Come

and gather yourselves together
unto the supper of the great God.

18. That ye may eat the flesh of
kings, and the flesh of captains,
and the flesh of mighty men, and
the flesh of horses, and of them
that sit on them, and the flesh of
all men, both free and bond, both
small and great.

19. And I saw the beast, and the
kings of the earth, and their
armies, gathered together to
make war against him that sat on
the horse, and against his army.

20. And the beast was taken, and
with him the false prophet that
was wrought miracles before
him, with which he deceived
them that had received the mark
of the beast, and them that
worshipped his image. These
both were cast alive into a lake of
fire burning with brimstone.

21. And the remnant were slain with the sword of him that sat upon the horse, which sword proceeded out of His mouth: and all the fowls were filled with their flesh.

***Here we are told, that not only will the nations be smitten with the sword, but the people of the world will be eaten up by the fowls of the air. They will eat the flesh of all the mighty men, the free and bond, the captains, and even the horses. As you can imagine, this will be a pretty gruesome scene within itself. The nations of the world will be gathered together and lead by the Antichrist to battle against Jesus and His Heavenly Army. After their defeat, the Antichrist, False Prophet, and everyone who caved into the New World Order System and accepted the Mark Of the Beast will be

thrown into the Lake Of Fire To burn for all
eternity.

Chapter 12

The New Jerusalem

After the people of the world have been Judged by Jesus, and rewarded with Heaven or Hell, a new heaven and a new earth will descend from Heaven. This is described in Revelations 21.

1. And I saw a new heaven and a new earth: for the first heaven and the first earth were passed away; and there was no more sea.

2. And I John saw the holy city, new Jerusalem, coming down from God out of Heaven, prepared as a bride adorned for her husband.

3. And I heard a great voice out of heaven saying, Behold, the tabernacle of God is with men, and he will dwell with them, and they shall be His people, and God Himself shall be with them, and be their God.

4. And God shall wipe away all tears from their eyes; and there shall be no more death, neither sorrow, nor crying, neither shall there be any more pain: for the former things are passed away.

5. And He that sat upon the throne said, Behold I make all things new, And He said unto me, Write: for these words are true and faithful.

6. And He said unto me, It is done. I am Alpha and Omega, the beginning and the end. I will give unto Him that is athirst of the fountain of the water of life freely.

7. He that overcometh shall inherit all things, and I will be his God, and he shall be My son.

8. But the fearful, and unbelieving, and the abominable, and murderers, and whoremongers, and sorcerers, and idolaters, and all liars, shall have their part in the lake which burneth

with fire and brimstone: which is the
second death.

*** God tells us in these scriptures that it is
during this time, after this present world has
been brought to an end and Judged, that He
Will dwell amongst His people. All of the
pain, suffering, and heartache that we
currently feel in this lifetime, will be no
more. We will always be surrounded by
God's Love and Joy, His Peace and
Happiness. All of the wars, terrorism, and
non-ending tragedies will cease to exist as
we live and thrive in Eternity with the
Almighty Creator of this Universe. God also
tells us in these scriptures, as He does in the
Alphabet, that He Is Indeed the "Alpha and
Omega, the beginning and the end", which
is represented in our Alphabet as the Letters
A and Z.

The Key to being a recipient of this, is that you must overcome this World, which God tells us in verse 7. What He means by this is that you must be cleansed and set free from Sin and Iniquity by the Blood Of Jesus. You must have endured Trials, Tribulation, and Persecution. You must be counted worthy to enter God's Kingdom. God is not going to allow just anybody to walk into His Kingdom without first meeting His requirements.

This is the pat where most of the people in the world stumble; everyone wants to go to Heaven on their own terms, or according to the terms of their belief system. And as God tells us in verse 8, people that Practice witchcraft/sorcery, worship false gods (fallen angels), liars, reject Jesus, and all of the other ungodly Practices /lifestyles, Will not Go to Heaven/ Will Not Inherit The Kingdom Of God. Most people reject those words from God and stumble in their emotions at God He speaks such things. They refuse to accept and believe in the severity of God; that He, who claims to be such a loving God, would actually cast people, His created beings, into the Lake Of Fire, to Burn for all eternity.

But I am here to tell you, dear people, yes indeed God Loves you, and is a loving God, and yes He wants dearly to have you in His Kingdom for all eternity. Having said this, He also has a standard by which He Judges human kind, on their worthiness to inherit His Kingdom. It is not God's Will that you Perish in your Sin(s) and Burn In Hell for all Eternity. It breaks His Heart when people die without first having His Only Begotten Son Jesus Christ as their Lord and Savior. He is not going to Force Himself on you to make you Believe in Him.

God is a gentle God a very heartfelt God, Genuine and soft spoken, when He wants to be. His ways are not our ways nor are our Thoughts His Thoughts. It is critical that people understand and grasp this. He is always watching and pondering the contents of our heart and our ways; every thought, action and word we speak is being recorded in Heaven and we all Will be held accountable and rewarded accordingly on the day of Judgment.

Made in the USA
Columbia, SC
14 December 2023

27869838R00074